ELLA

A DOG WITH A JOB

BASED ON A TRUE STORY

WRITTEN BY
AJ CULLEN

ILLUSTRATED BY
KALLIE FRIESEN

ajcullen978@gmail.com

FIRST EDITION

My dearest Cinderella "ELLA" Cullen,

You have touched more lives than you know. My hope is that you will continue to do so through telling your story. Thank you for all of the love and laughter you brought to everyone around you.

Bonjour! I'm ELLA, a dog with a job. Actually, come to think of it, I have had many jobs.

Ella's Resume

I have been working my whole life. My first job was as an emotional support animal to my human, AJ. AJ gave me a forever home when she was in college, and don't tell anyone, but she snuck me in and out of her dorm room for many months. She says I'm the troublemaker! Woof!

Shh!
Woof
Woof

You're probably wondering what an emotional support animal is. It was my job to help AJ when she was feeling sad, scared, or lonely. AJ really needed my help so I made it my mission to always make her smile, and to sit near her when she was scared or worried. I didn't really have to work very hard at this, for it was just in my nature.

HELLO

As time went on, AJ got stronger, and it was time for me to find my next job. You'll never believe this, but my first paying job was at a gourmet dog bakery!! A nice human hired not only AJ, but ME TOO! While AJ was busy using something called a cash register, I worked hard earning my salary of dog bones. Let me tell you it wasn't easy. I had to do things like taste the treats (you know, for quality control) greet customers at the door, and act as the store security dog, making sure no birds or mysterious UPS men got too close.

PUPCAKES
VANILLA $4
CHOCOLATE $4
PEANUT BUTTER $4
LAVENDER $4

Other than my role in quality control, I am most proud of helping AJ create the Autism Barks fundraiser, where we sold gourmet puzzle piece dog treats to raise awareness for autism. I also volunteered with AJ as the official mascot of an autism charity AJ and her friends started at their college. This job didn't pay me a lot of bones, but I got LOTS of love and attention, and sometimes, customers would even buy the puzzle piece treats for me!

AUTISIM
AWARENESS

AJ and I loved working at the dog bakery, and with all the bones we earned, AJ started taking me to dog school. AJ and I worked hard to become a pet therapy team. I loved helping AJ and sharing joy with all the dog bakery customers, and AJ knew I could bring joy and love to many more.

Dog school was tough!! There were so many humans and so many dogs in my class. I made many friends. One day, my friend, Boo, invited me over to practice for an upcoming test.

When AJ finally took my leash off, after babbling something about good behavior, I got a glimpse of a giant ocean in Boo's backyard. I ran right over to it and dove on in. I took a nice swim in what I later found out was called a "pool." AJ was not happy with me, but luckily, Boo's human thought it was very funny.

After I did some ACTUAL studying and practice with AJ and my other human friends, it was time for me to take my test and become a therapy dog. Not long after I passed my test, AJ finished something humans call college. AJ and I decided it was time for us to move back to Massachusetts where AJ's human family lived. I was very sad to leave my great job at the Dipidy Dawg, but as long as I was with AJ, I knew we'd be okay. AJ,my grandfather, and I drove ALL the way from Florida to Massachusetts. I had to help my grandfather drive most of the way and help them find the best spots along the route to find good bacon.

When we got to Massachusetts, AJ began working as a special education teacher, and because of my therapy dog training, I was hired too! Boy, did I love this job, almost as much as bacon. This job used a lot of the skills I used before as AJ's emotional support animal. It was my job to help the kids who were sad, angry, or hurting in some way. Sometimes, when the kids were too sad to talk to me, they would do something called "email" me. AJ helped me to respond to each and every email, as it's hard to type with no thumbs! I spent a lot of time in AJ's classroom, and I made many good friends.

A B C D E
A a

For some crazy reason, AJ decided it was time to move to Cape Cod, Massachusetts, and we were on the hunt again for another new job. AJ was hired to work in group homes for adults with disabilities. This was another job I LOVED. At this job, I helped to motivate my human friends to exercise, and we got to go on walks all over breath-taking Cape Cod. One time, they even took me on the ferry to Martha's Vineyard! I also helped to teach my human friends about responsibility, with many of them helping AJ in caring for me.

You'll never guess what happened next, we moved AGAIN. It's good thing I love to explore as much as AJ did. Not too long after we moved, AJ found us a new job at a nursing home. I had a funny feeling when we pulled up on the first day, knowing it smelled familiar. When we got inside, I sniffed up and down and dragged AJ all around. Finally, I looked around and remembered, This is where my great grandmother had lived! Oh boy, was I happy to be there. My great-grandmother always gave the best snacks, and her roommates always left crumbs on the floor. It was sad to remember that my great-grandmother was in heaven, but I was so happy to know I was working here in her honor.

ASSISTED
LIVING

As before, I made friends quickly there! I had never met so many dog lovers. Not only did I help the patients, but I also became good friends with AJ's coworkers. My job here was very busy. I was always on the go, visiting with patients and their families, cleaning the crumbs off the floor, and making sure the giant vacuum didn't get too close to any of my friends. AJ brought me to see patients and their families who were sad or sick, and I always made sure to bring them lots of love and laughter. AJ also brought me to spend time with residents who had loved and lost their own dogs, and residents who missed their dogs that were back at home.

MARCH
happy Spring!

When I wasn't busy spending time with my friends, I helped AJ with something she called paperwork and meetings. Meetings were a real snooze; I just wanted to be with my friends! Sometimes though, if the meetings were important, I would make sure not to snore, and listen to what was going on.

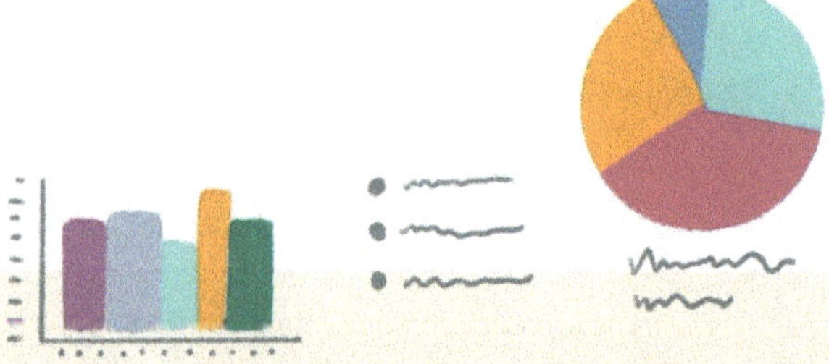

After working in the nursing home, I got word that it was time for me to get promoted. It was time for me to become an angel! I was very sad to leave AJ and all of the many friends I had made during my time on earth, but I knew it was my time to go and help people both on earth and in heaven. While AJ and the humans were very sad about my promotion, I knew I could do more for people by gaining my angel wings and watching over them from above.

I can be with AJ, at the dog bakery, in the classroom, and at the nursing home all at the same time with my angel wings. As an angel, I can fly, bringing love and joy to more areas than I could while on earth. Now I can share the stories of my work life and all of the fun adventures I had with AJ with all of my new friends in heaven. Don't get me wrong, I miss all of my friends on earth, two and four-legged alike, but I know that being an angel is the most important job I have been given. Becoming an angel isn't sad; it's rewarding and fun. I will miss all of my human friends, but I will always be with them and will never stop bringing them happiness and love.

PUPCAKES
VANILLA $4
CHOCOLATE $4
PEANUT BUTTER $4
LAVENDER $4

ASSISTED LIVING

HELLO

HANG IN THERE
A B C D E F
A a

Ella

Meet AJ Cullen, Ella's owner and friend, who continues her legacy to this day by telling her story to all who will listen. AJ has taken an active role in organizing events and assisting in raising autism awareness on a community and national level. Currently, AJ is training Lola, a black Labrador, as a future therapy animal and hopes that Ella's impact through her life and the pages of this book will continue far into the future and inspire others in this noble calling.

CPSIA information can be obtained
at www.ICGtesting.com
Printed in the USA
BVHW061414180321
602893BV00007B/860

9 780578 726632